"Nature gave us the correct recipe."
Michael Braungart & William McDonough
(The Upcycle, North Point Press, 2013, p.221)

"The world will not evolve past its current state of crisis by
using the same thinking that created the situation."
Albert Einstein
(as quoted in: *Cradle to Cradle* by Michael Braungart &
William McDonough, Vintage, 2009)

FULL CYCLES ONLY!

Written by
George Hohbach & Ehrengard Hohbach
with Scott Marcano

Based on the life of Michael Braungart
including his books
Cradle to Cradle: Remaking the Way We Make Things
and *The Upcycle*

1st Edition

© 2022 George Hohbach & Ehrengard Hohbach

Project Management: Scott Marcano, Diablo Productions

In anticipation of the Cradle to Cradle novels, George and Ehrengard planted 1000 trees in California in 2019 with the Environmental Charity *One Tree Planted*.
10 percent of the authors' (George & Ehrengard) revenue from each sale of the book go to the *Cradle to Cradle NGO*.

Authorization: Michael Braungart has approved Concept and Book and authorizes use of his name and copyrighted materials for inclusion and reference in Book.

Bibliographical Information of the Deutsche Nationalbibliothek
This publication is listed in the Deutsche Nationalbibliographie of the Deutsche Nationalbibliothek; detailed bibliographical information can be accessed under http: //dnb.d-nb.de

Printing and Production: BoD – Books on Demand, Norderstedt

ISBN: 978-3-7562-9968-3

C2C GALAXY
-FULL CYCLES ONLY-

Concept by
George Hohbach
Story by
George Hohbach & Michael Braungart

Written by
George Hohbach & Ehrengard Hohbach
with Scott Marcano

Illustrations by
Juan Romera

Illustrations of Part 2, Michael Cartoon & Title Sequence, Photos as well as Music
& Lyrics of the Songs *C2C GALAXY & C2C CIRCULAR ECONOMY*
by
George Hohbach

Arrangement of the Songs and Sheet Music by
Alfred Huff

English Translation of Part 2
George Hohbach with Robin Palmer, author of the acclaimed Middle Grade book
series *Yours Truly, Lucy B. Parker*

CONTENTS

PART 1

C2C GALAXY
-FULL CYCLES ONLY-

PART 2

About Michael Braungart & Cradle to Cradle

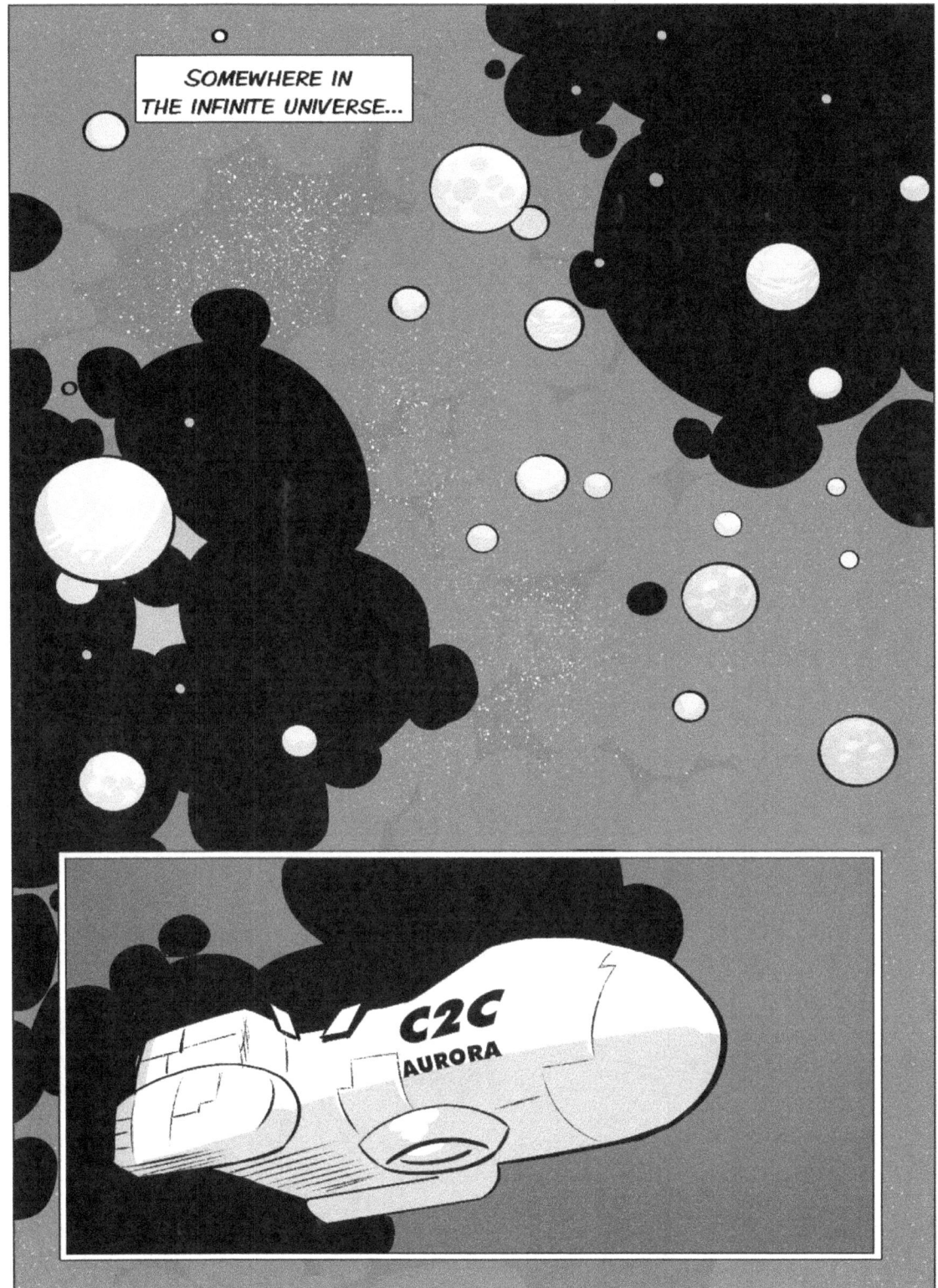

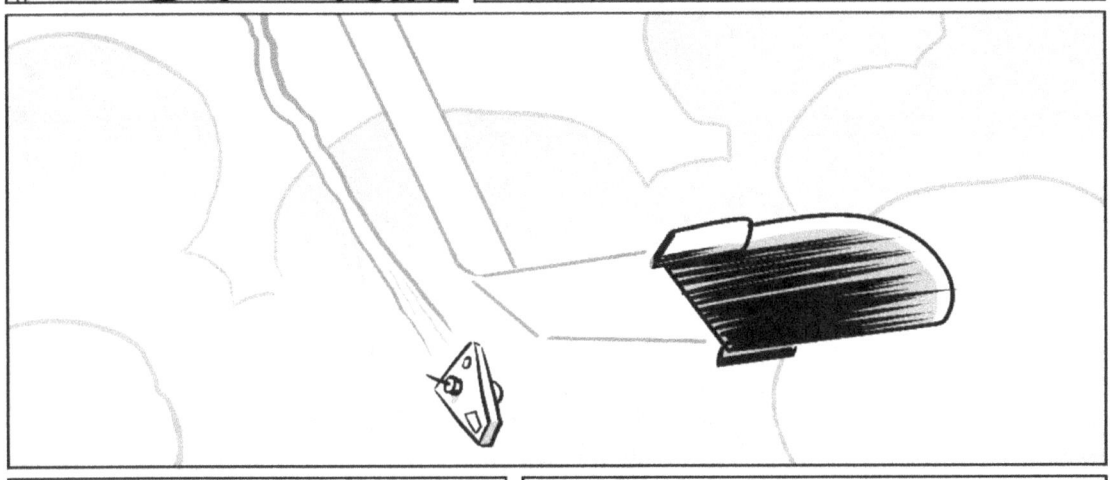

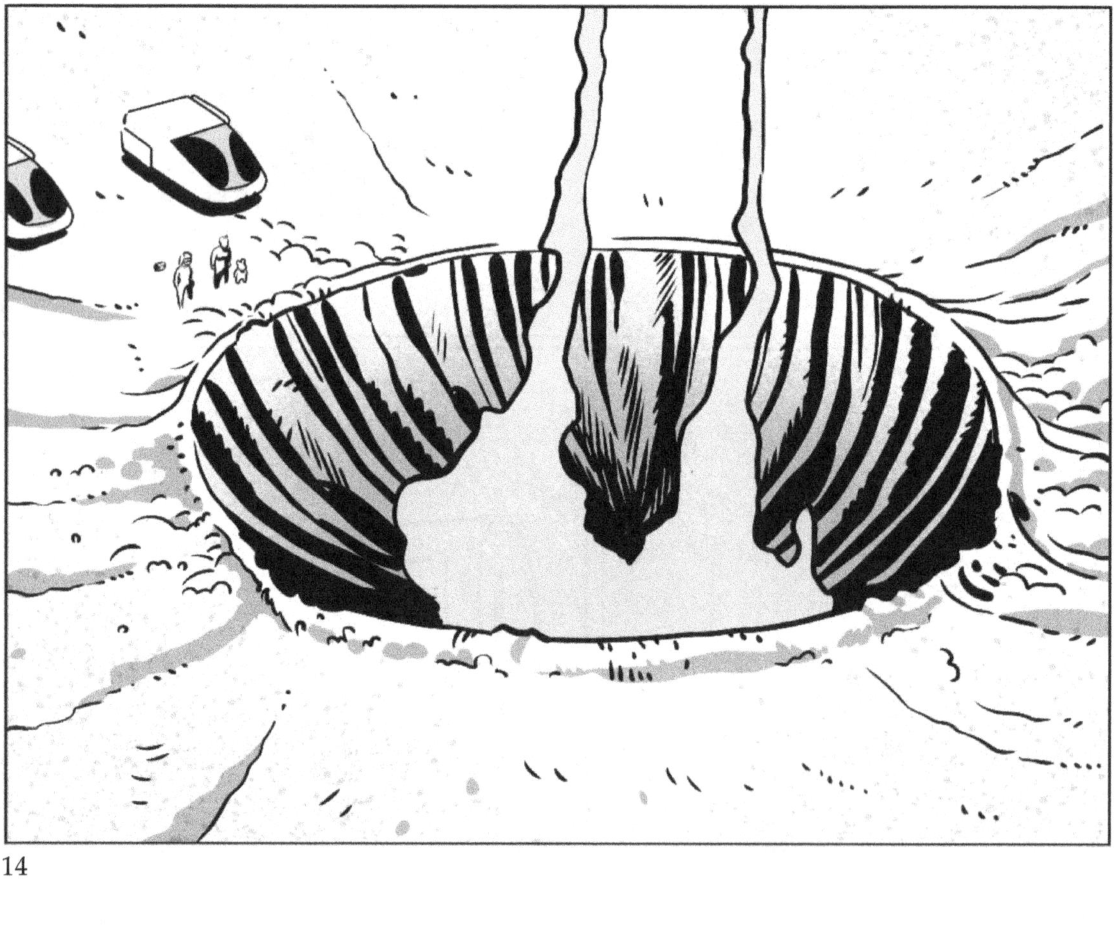

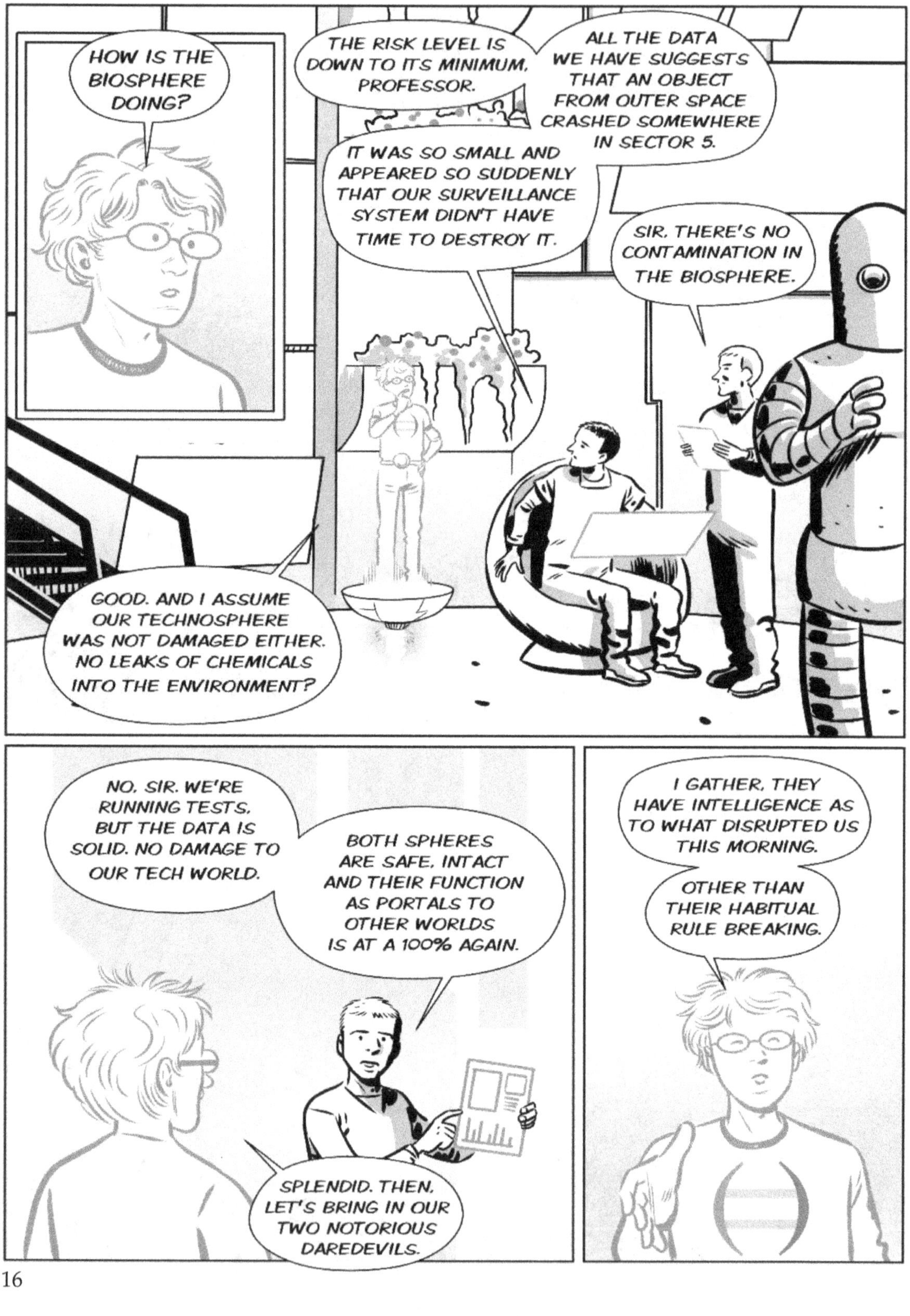

THANK YOU, PROFESSOR.

THAT WAS MOST INSPIRING, SIR.

JUST CALL ME MICHAEL.

WHAT, SIR, PROFESSOR--

--THAT WOULD BE AGAINST THE RULES.

OH, REALLY? NOW YOU CARE?! RELAX. TELL ME WHAT YOU KNOW ABOUT THE OBJECT THAT CRASHED ON AURORA TODAY.

WELL SIR... I MEAN, UM, "MICHAEL" WE RAN SEVERAL TESTS, AND IT TURNS OUT, THE OBJECT IS MADE OUT OF XERANIUM T1.

THAT'S ODD... THE SPACESHIP THAT LANDED ON AURORA 300 YEARS AGO WAS MADE OUT OF NANOTUBES CONSISTING OF XERANIUM T1 TOO.

THAT SUBSTANCE IS EXTREMELY RARE IN ALL THE KNOWN UNIVERSES.

DO YOU THINK, THE OBJECT WAS PART OF A SPACECRAFT?
IF SO, NOT A VERY HAPPY ONE, I'D SAY.
WHAT'S THE FILE NUMBER?
123-01

IT'S SO GREAT THAT QUANTUM COMPUTERS ARE HONEST.
OBJECT LIKELY MADE BY INTELLIGENT SPECIES. PURPOSE NOT KNOWN
I GUESS. WE'LL EITHER NEVER KNOW, OR JUST HAVE TO WAIT UNTIL WE FIND A NEW CLUE--

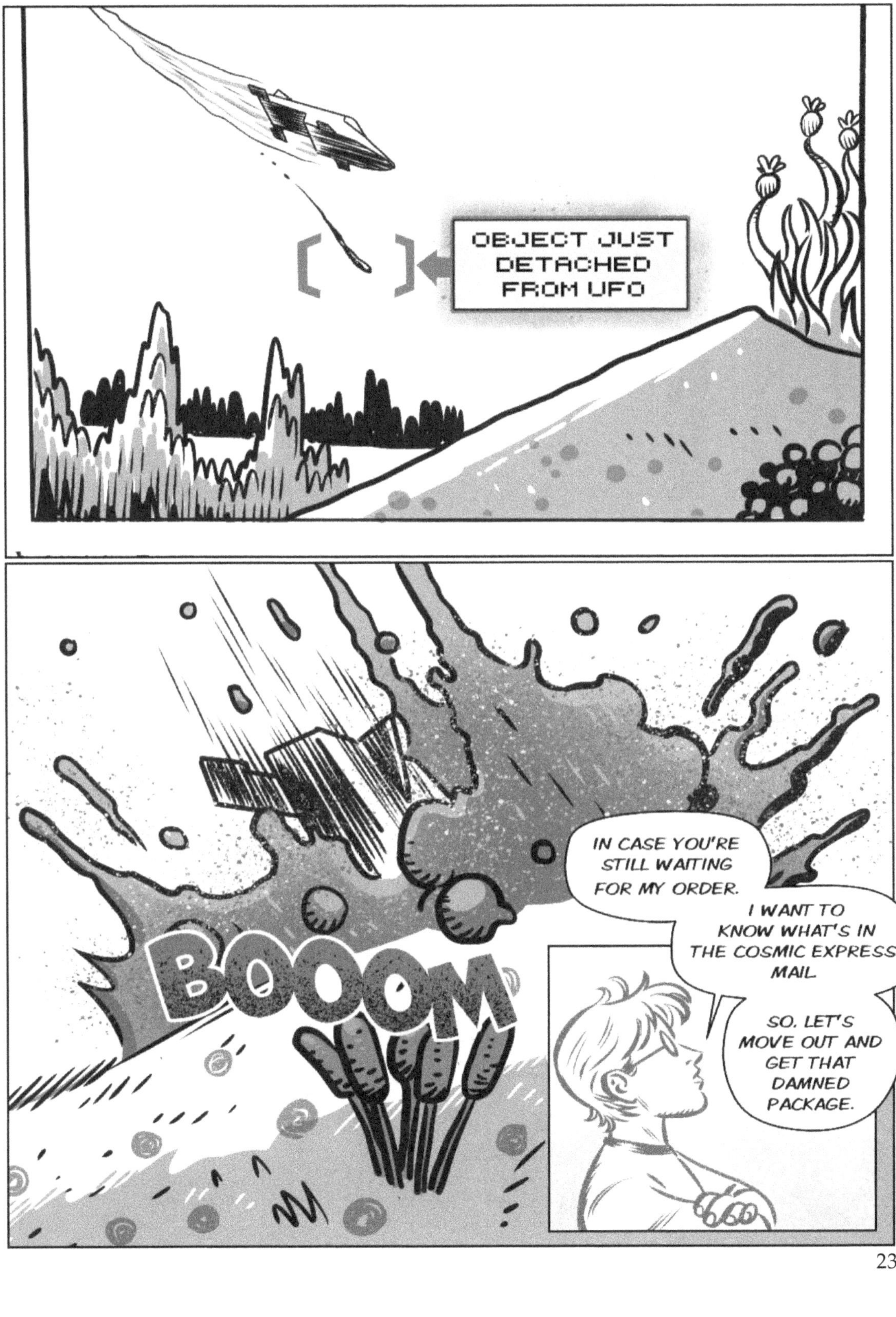

24

YOU CAN GET OFF MY SHOULDER NOW, YOU BRAVE LITTLE PUFF-BALL MY SHOULDER IS NOT YOUR PRIVATE VIP BOX TO CHILL AND--

--DEFINITELY NOT TO... PEE ON. OH, MAN!

BEING AN INTERGALACTIC NANNY IS A TOUGH JOB, BOB. MY HEART SO GOES OUT TO YOU.

OH, SHUT UP! I REALLY SHOULDN'T HAVE TO DO... THIS! I DON'T EVEN KNOW WHY THIS ALIEN FURBALL THINKS WE'RE BESTIES.

MAYBE IT THINKS YOU HAVE A CUTE BUTT. DO YOU WORK OUT A LOT?

REALLY? THAT'S THE BEST YOU CAN COME UP WITH?

THAT'S SO LAME, EVEN THE MARMOT FEELS BAD FOR YOU

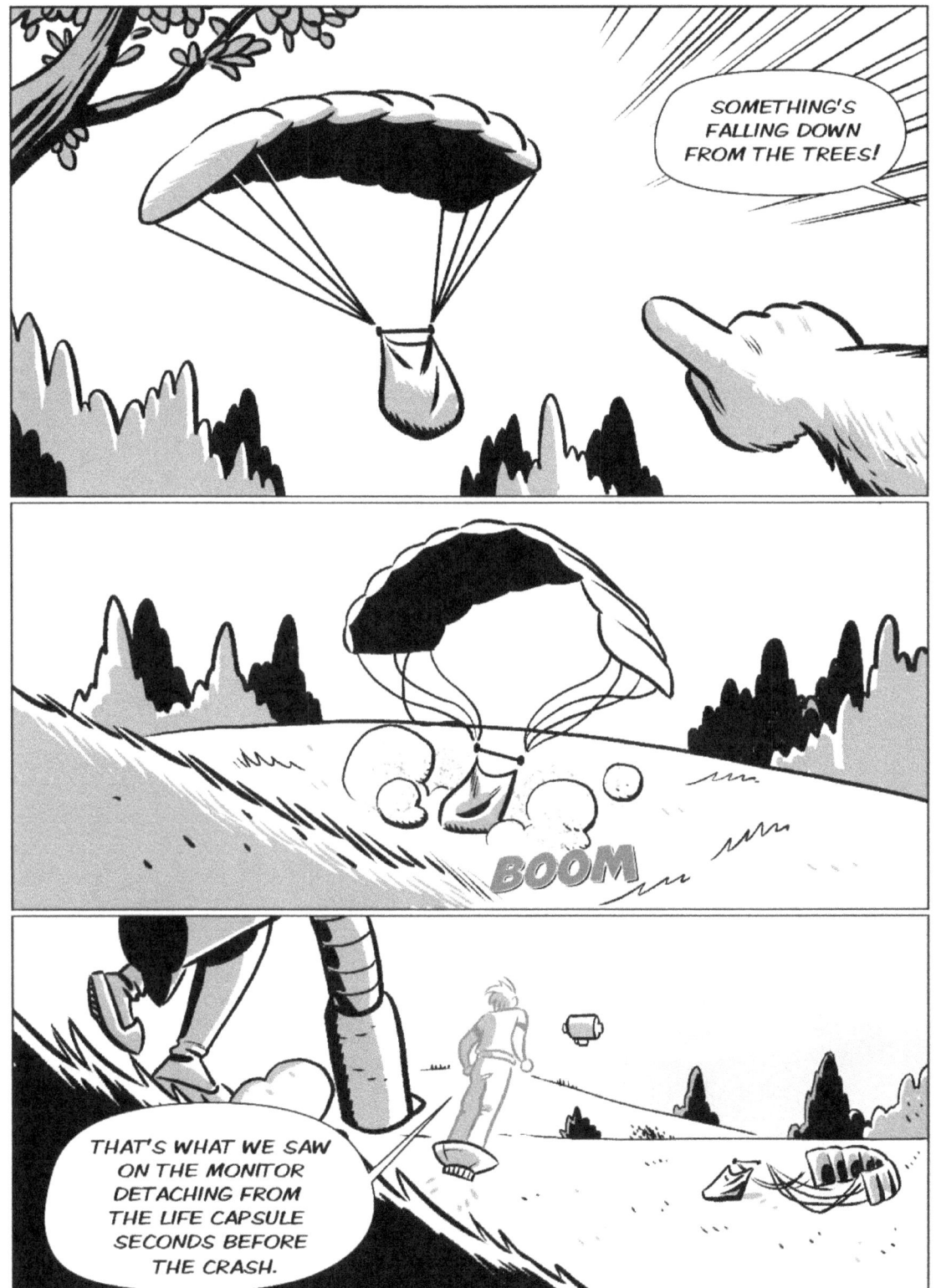

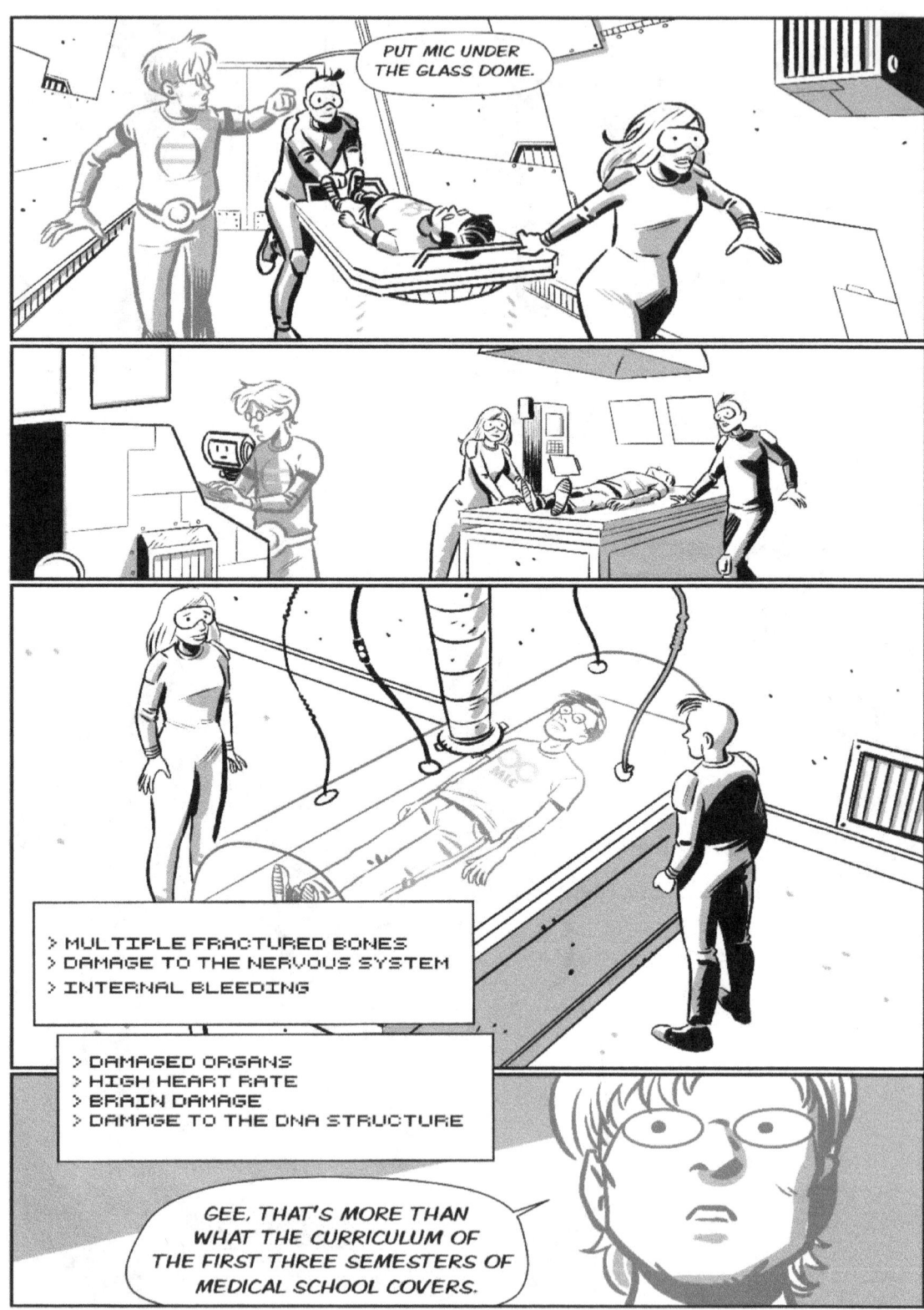

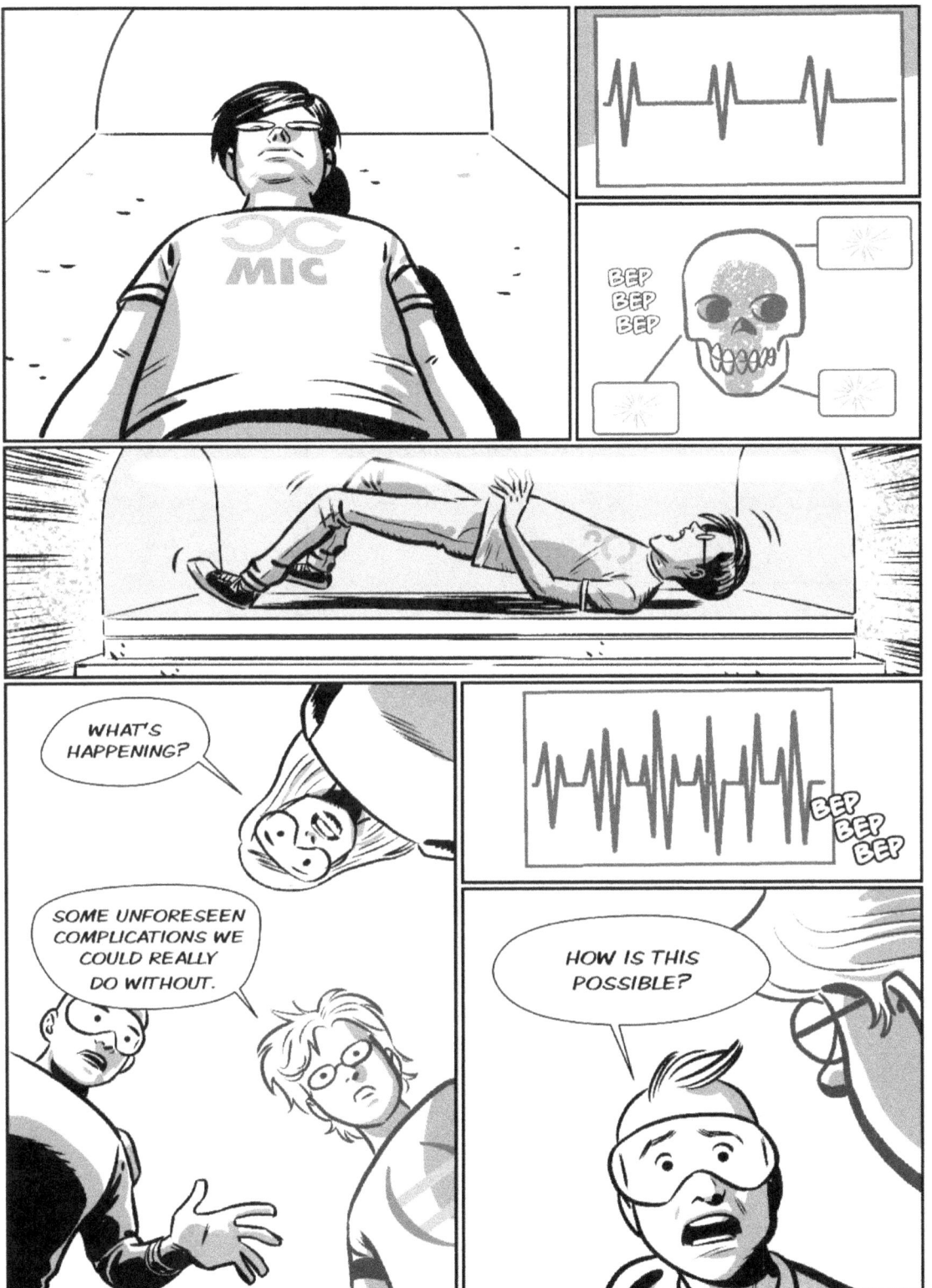

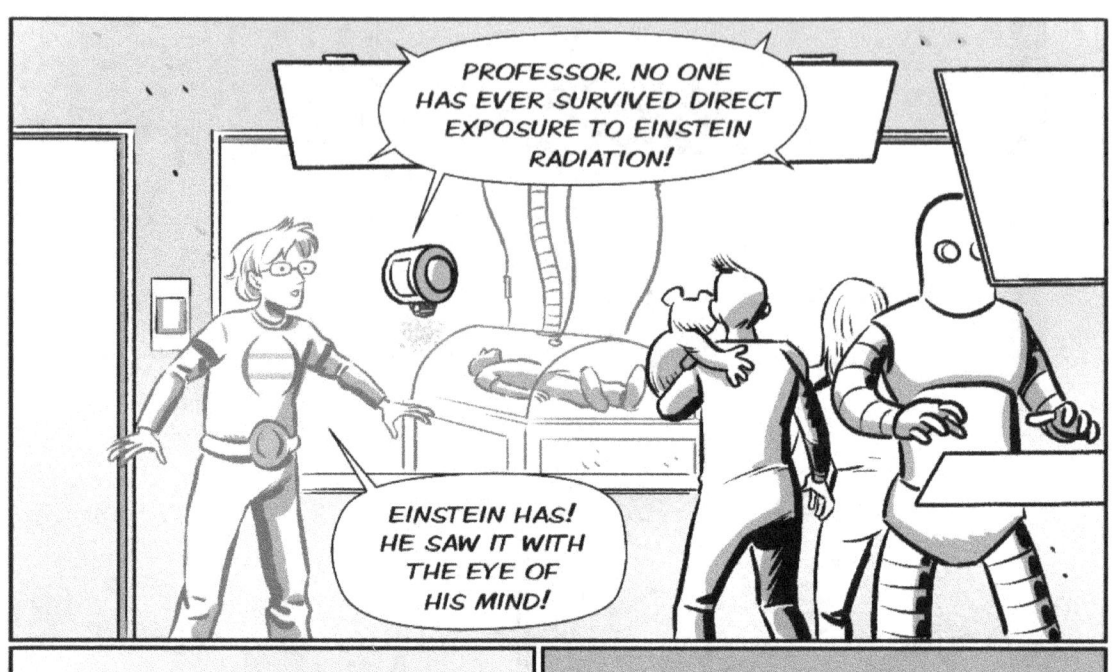

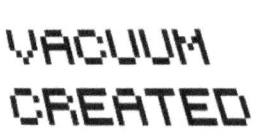

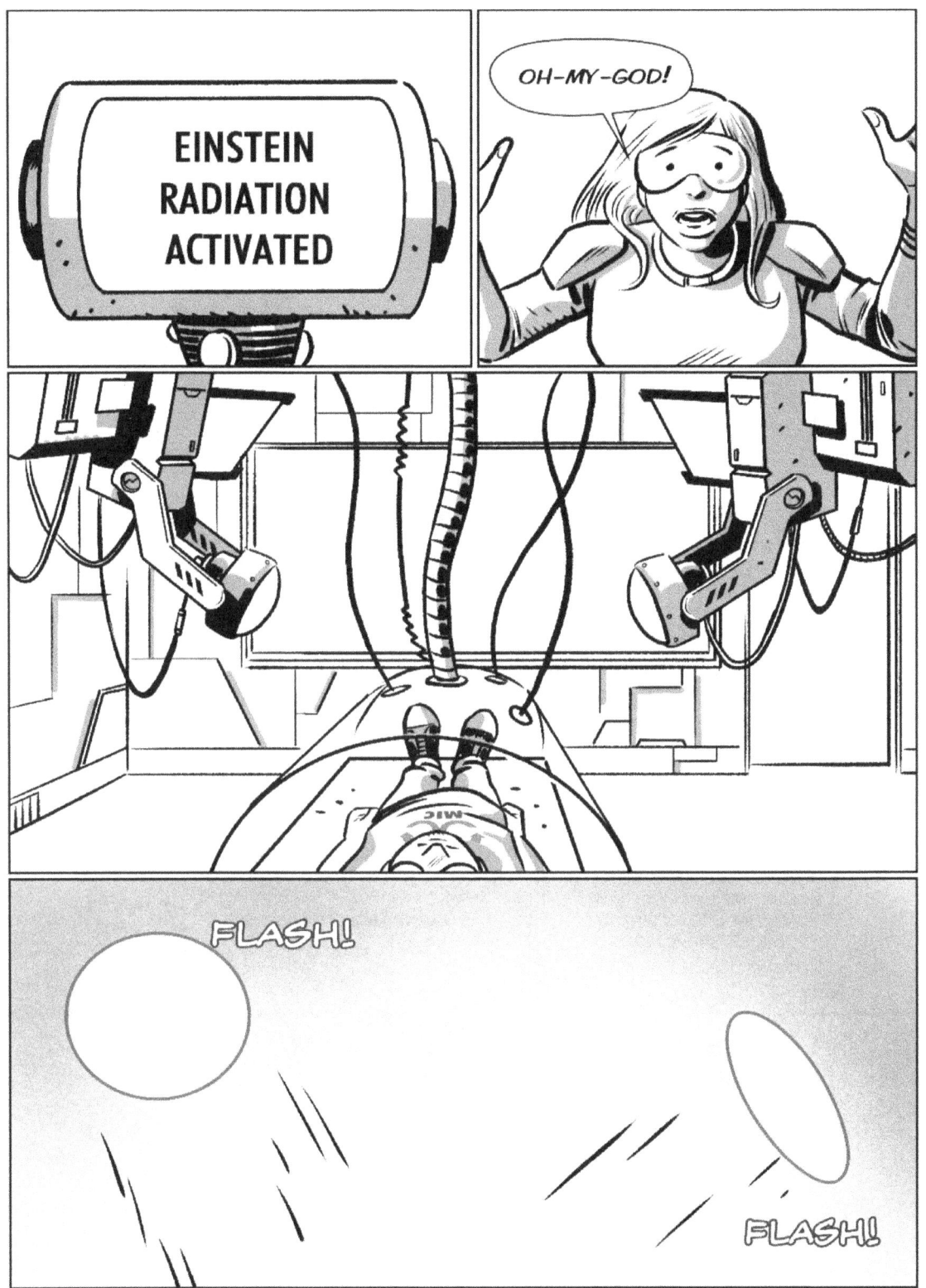

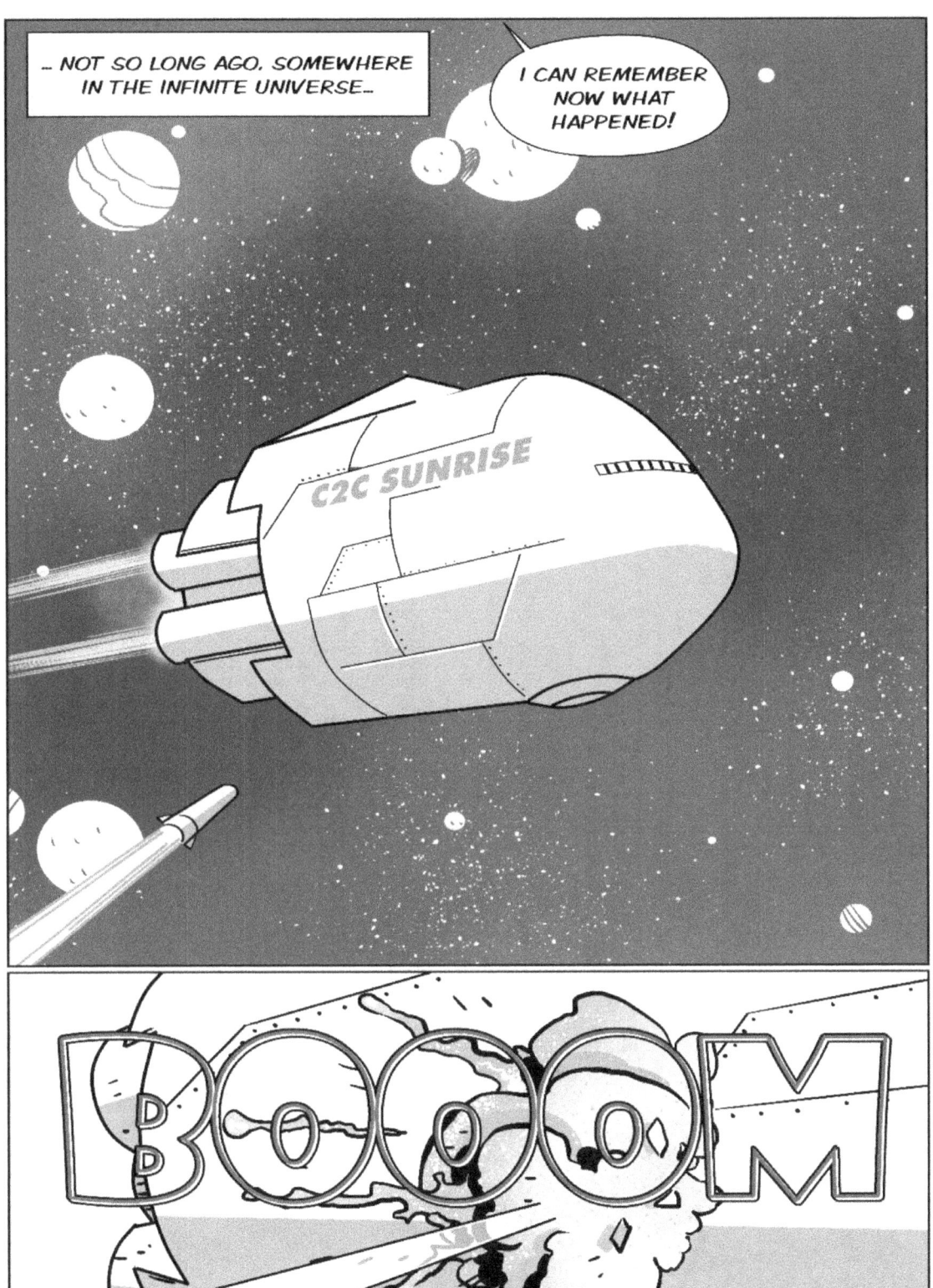

49

PLANET EARTH, 350 YEARS AGO

WHAT IS IT?

THE LATEST CRADLE TO CRADLE SMART ASTRONAUT T-SHIRT WE DEVELOPED WITH NASA AND ORLANDO MCKAY. YOUR FAVOURITE FASHION DESIGNER.

LOOK!

WHAT IS THAT?

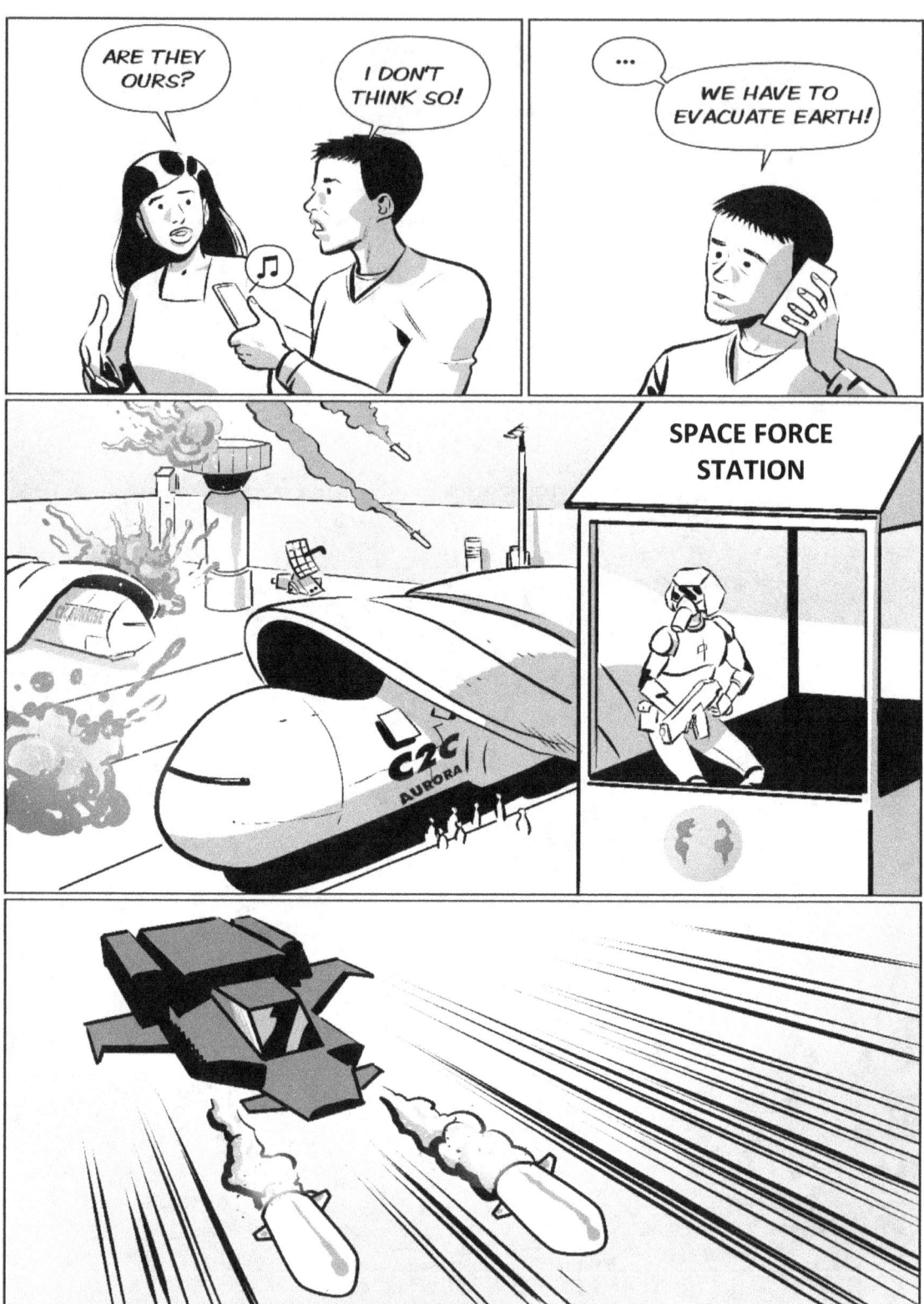

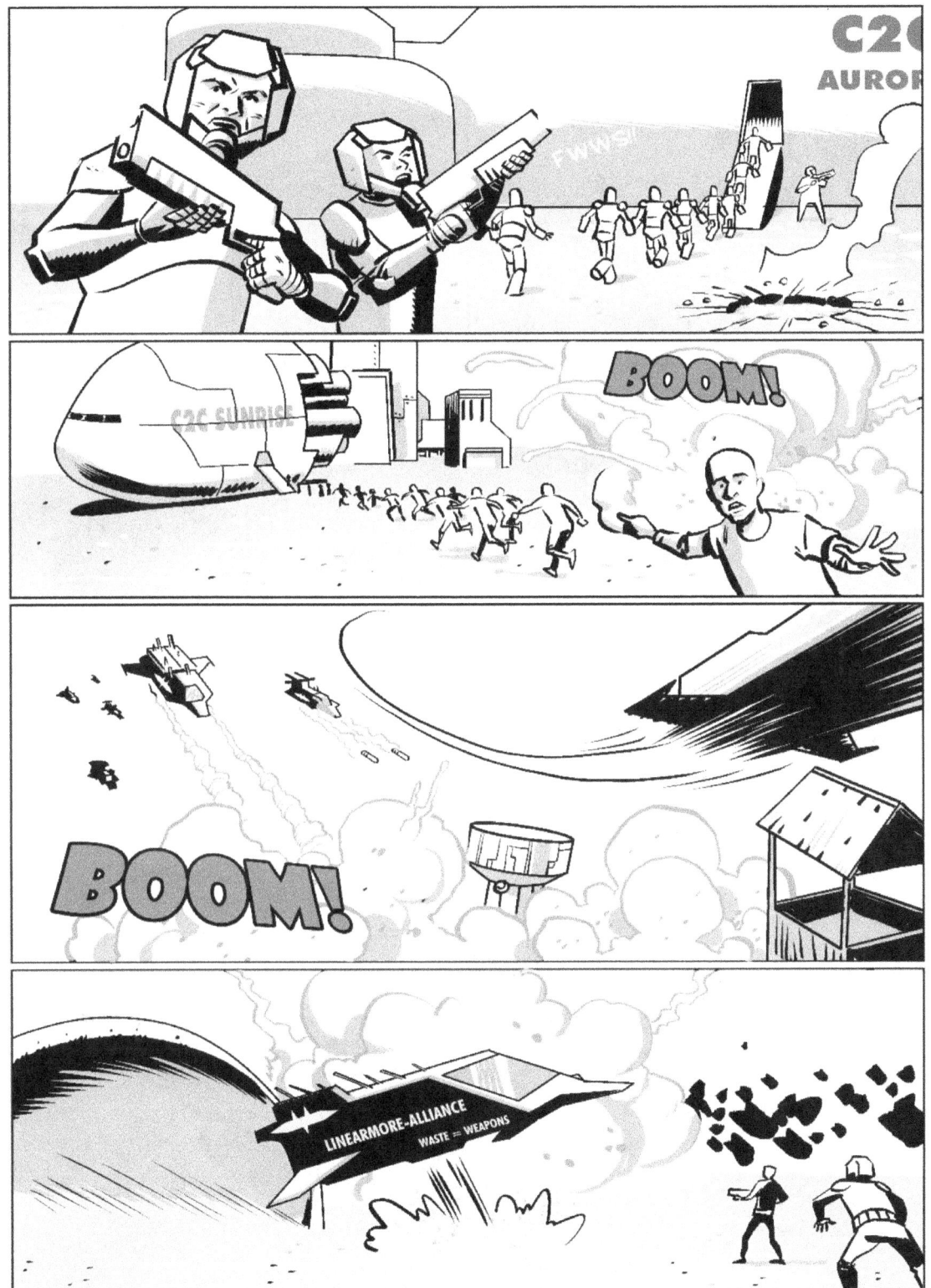

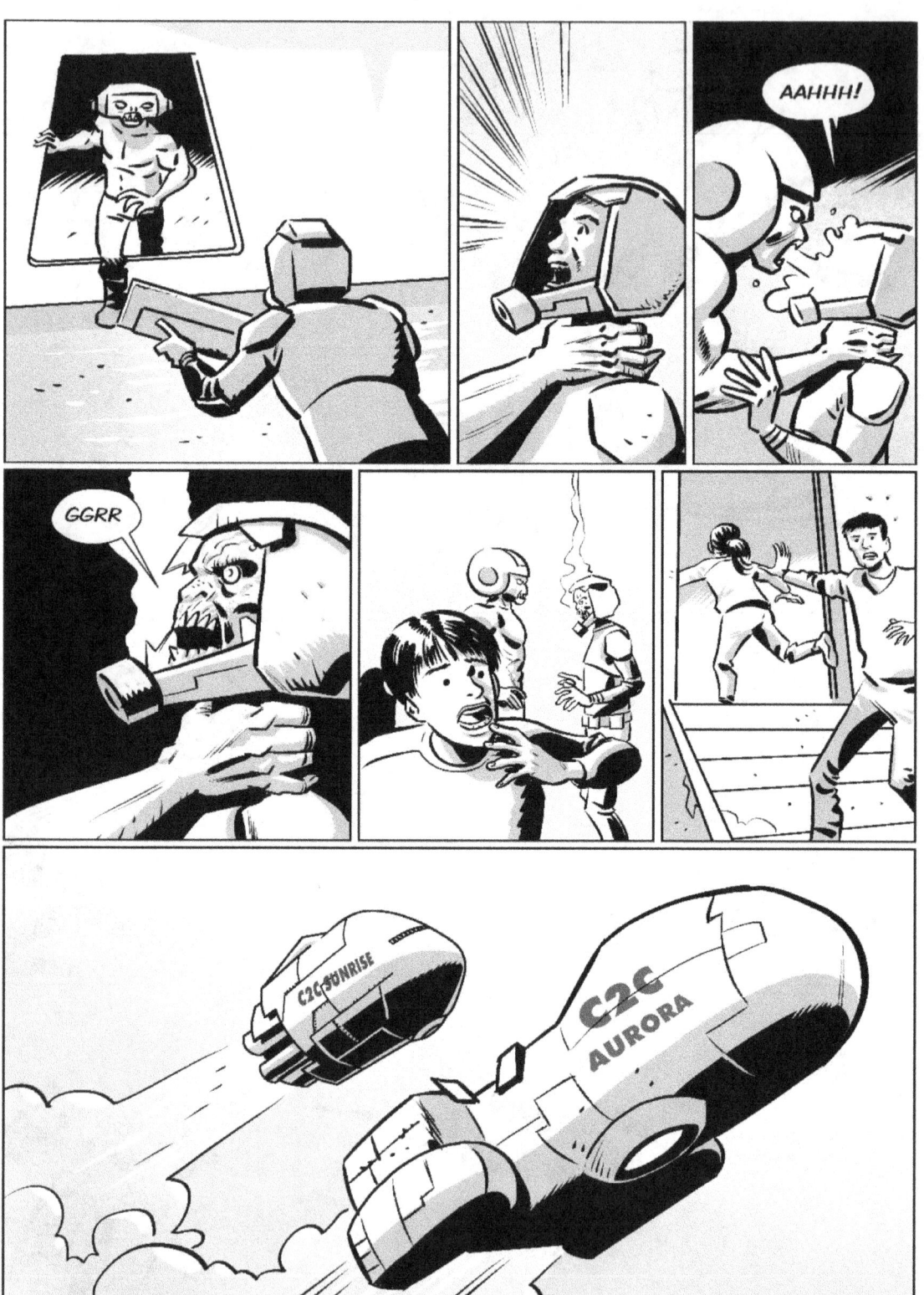

WE HAD JUST MANAGED TO AVOID THE WORST OF CLIMATE CHANGE ON EARTH, SUCKING CO2 OUT OF THE AIR WITH ARTIFICIAL TREES AND THE LIKE.

WE HAD CONVERTED OUR ECONOMY TO A C2C CIRCULAR ECONOMY WHEN THE LINEARMORE-ALLIANCE ATTACKED US.

MY DAD, THE LEADING C2C SCIENTIST, WAS SUPPOSED TO COME TO AURORA WITH US AND THE OTHERS 300 YEARS LATER, WHEN YOU GUYS WOULD HAVE BUILT A BLOSSOMING C2C CITY.

OUR MISSION WAS TO TELL YOU ABOUT YOUR HISTORY, WHERE YOU'RE FROM, WHY YOU'RE HERE.

BUT NOW, IT LOOKS LIKE I'M BRINGING THE WORST PARTS OF THE PAST WITH ME TO AURORA.

THE LINEARMORE-ALLIANCE SOMEHOW WAS ABLE TO FIND THE C2C SUNRISE AND DESTROY IT. I ONLY KNOW THAT I ESCAPED BARELY, AND I'M SURE, THEY'LL FIND PLANET AURORA NOW, TOO.

I SHOULD NEVER HAVE COME HERE, NEVER!

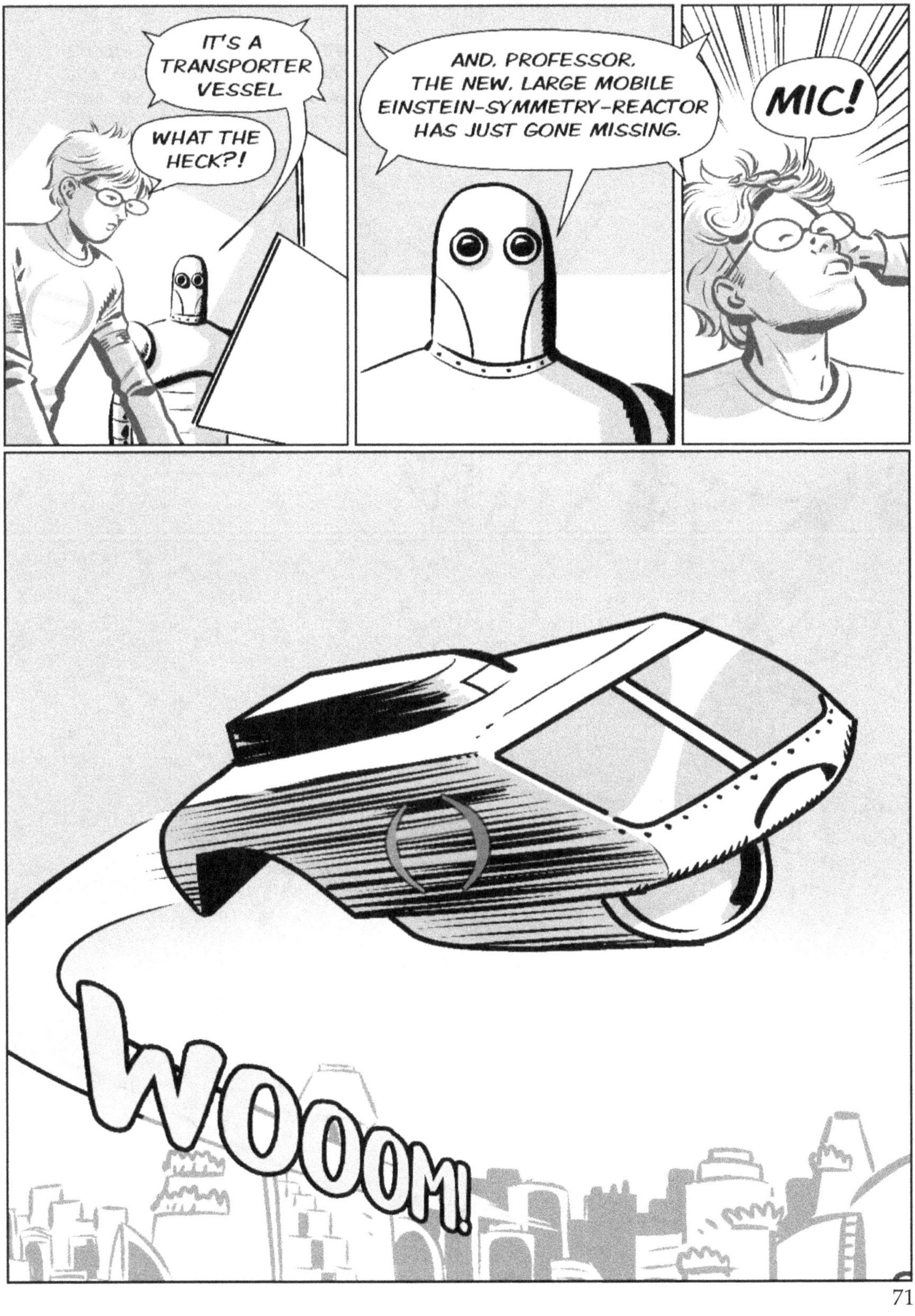

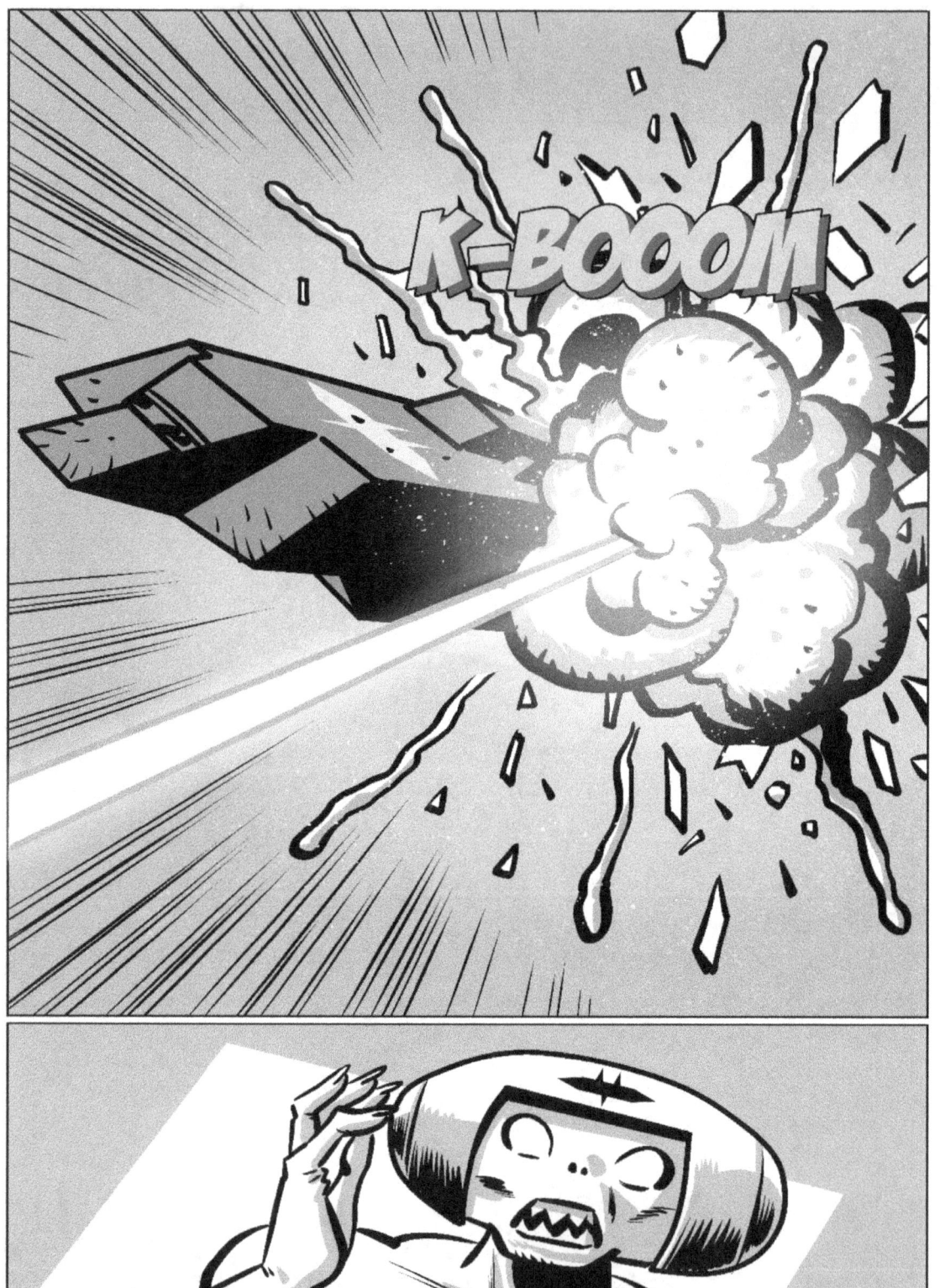

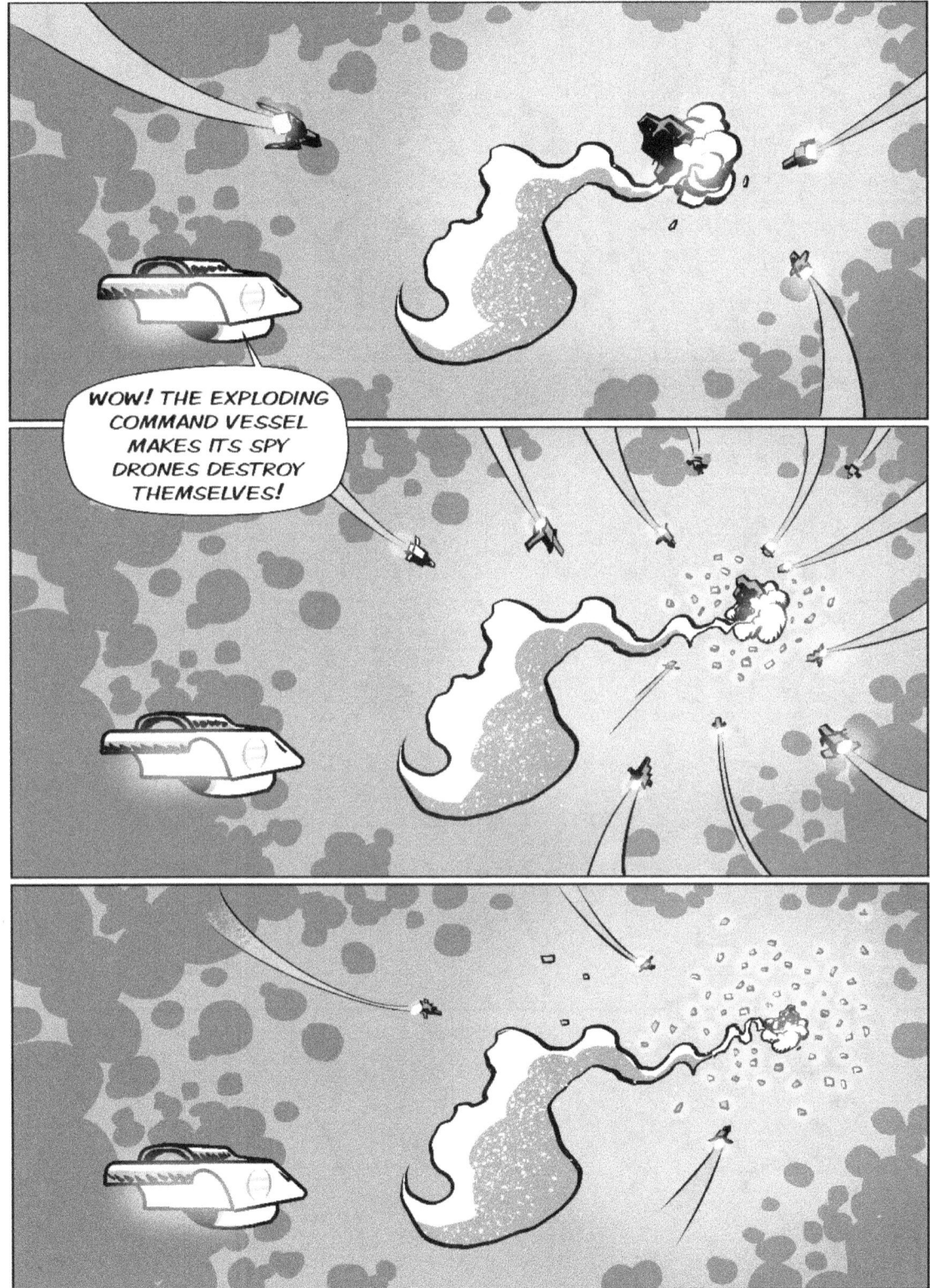

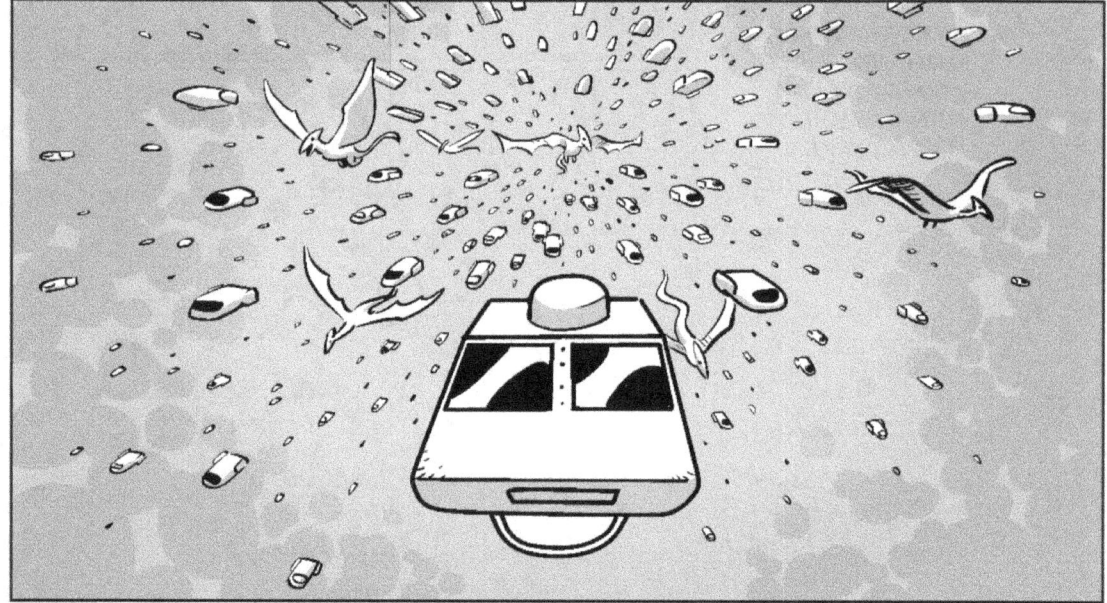

C2C GALAXY

Title Song to the Graphic Novel

Music & lyrics: George Hohbach
Arrangement: Alfred Huff

Intro

Melody

Verse

We see the good   And de-fine   Po - si - tive   The way we li-

ve.   We see it all   As a whole   Po - si - tive   The lea-ding

Bridge

role   We live   gi-ving More while li-ving   From the start   The whole at heart.

Chorus

C   2   C   Ga - la-xy   Na-ture's way   as meant to

be   C   2   C   we are,   we are,   we are.   C   2   C

 # C2C GALAXY

VERSE 1
We see the good
And define
Positive
The way we live.

We see it all
As a whole
Positive
The leading role.

BRIDGE
We live giving
More while living
From the start
The whole at heart.

CHORUS
C2C Galaxy
Nature's way as meant to be
C2C
We are, we are, we are.

C2C is our core
Symmetry comes to the fore
C2C
We are, we are, we are.

VERSE 2
We build on cycles
Abundance in mind

Society
Constructively

We strive for more
More good for all
One planet
Where we stand tall

BRIDGE
We make it better
Now and forever
Innovation
A celebration.

CHORUS
C2C Galaxy
Nature's way as meant to be
C2C
We are, we are, we are.

C2C is our core
Symmetry comes to the fore
C2C
We are, we are, we are.

C2C CIRCULAR ECONOMY

Music & lyrics: George Hohbach
Arrangement: Alfred Huff

C2C CIRCULAR ECONOMY

VERSE 1
The C2C Footprint
Can occur
With open-source information
To locally spur
Creation
Innovation
That is positive across each nation

BRIDGE
No more extraction
But creation at a fraction
Of the cost
No more resources will be lost

CHORUS
Communication
Transportation
Keep resources in circulation
Abundance, celebration
Welcome pure creation
C2C, C2C, Circular Economy

VERSE 2
The C2C Footprint
Has a chance
With the Circular Economy
Living C2C's balance
Creation
Innovation
Nature's recipe across each nation

BRIDGE
No more extraction
But creation at a fraction
Of the cost
People & Planet can benefit the most

CHORUS
Communication
Transportation
Keep resources in circulation
Abundance, celebration
Welcome pure creation
C2C, C2C, Circular Economy
C2C, C2C,
Circular Economy

PART 2

About
Michael Braungart
& Cradle to Cradle
with illustrations and photos by George Hohbach

BIOSPHERE

POSITIVE

TECHNOSPHERE

POSITIVE

MICHAEL CYCLE

Why the Cradle to Cradle design concept makes companies, people and governments partners in striving for eco-intelligent, climate-smart solutions

MICHAEL BRAUNGART, who is the source of inspiration with his life and ideas for this book, is a world-renowned chemistry professor who has taught at several U.S. institutions, including Carnegie Mellon University in Pittsburgh, Pennsylvania and the Darden Business School in  Charlottesville, Virginia. He is the founder and CEO of EPEA, the international Environmental Protection Encouragement Agency, co-author of two international bestsellers and co-founder of the groundbreaking, *eco-intelligent and climate-smart* CRADLE TO CRADLE design concept. He developed this thought-leading idea with his U.S. partner and co-author, the pioneering environmental architect William McDonough. Internationally, Cradle to Cradle is usually known by the abbreviation C2C. The philosophy and school of thought of

Cradle to Cradle stands for the following: high-quality materials of a product are fully reused again when a product reaches the end of its usability cycle (end-of-use). This is in stark contrast to the linear thinking of "Cradle to Grave" (take-make-waste) which signifies that products, which have reached the end of their usefulness are either immediately thrown away to become waste, which generally pollutes the environment, including the emissions of greenhouse gases, and causes valuable raw materials to get lost, or, through the downcycling of the ingredients of the product, the materials increasingly lose their quality and then (just a little later) must also be disposed of as waste. Michael Braungart, along with his American partner William McDonough—with whom he founded the C2C-consulting firm MBDC in Charlottesville, Virginia and the Cradle to Cradle Products Innovation Institute in San Francisco, California—has received numerous international awards for his groundbreaking work benefitting human society on a global scale including the U.S. Environmental Protection Agency's "Presidential

Green Chemistry Challenge Award" in 2003. In 2007, *Time* magazine named both Michael Braungart and William McDonough "Heroes of the Environment". With the revolutionary Cradle to Cradle design concept, companies around the globe are more and more succeeding in continuously reusing innovative, increasingly safe materials of the highest quality in biological and technical cycles. Using energy-effective and efficient eco-intelligent and climate-smart production processes—based on, e.g., utilizing ever more renewable, local energy, saving energy via reusing precious materials or keeping carbon contained in the recycled substance—ensures, at a progressive rate, that all used, valuable substances and production processes in both the biosphere and the technosphere are **permanently safe from the outset**. Thus, the process creates more and more positive effects for people and the environment, and ensures that resources are handled responsibly. Therefore, short-term thinking and long-term oriented actions are supposed to get united constructively and innovatively, just as the smallest levels (the molecules, the individual human being) and the larger levels (nature, the planet) are brought into greater harmony. The goal of Cradle to Cradle is to present the positive-holistic unity pattern of nature in the form of a simple, highly effective (eco-effective) and also efficient approach to mankind. This allows each individual human being to create a growing **POSITIVE FOOTPRINT** on the planet, since the Cradle to Cradle design concept, from the start, makes all materials and production processes safer and more conducive for planet and people, and aims for continuous improvement—including solutions for climate change.

This is one of the central, socially relevant topics of the present and future of humanity, and the Cradle to Cradle community continues to grow steadily across the planet. With Cradle to Cradle, the concept of the modern "circular economy" has been defined cyclically and positively with nutrient cycles in a consistent fashion, and linked to the idea of continuous, comprehensive global improvement and upcycling. Today, numerous international organizations, such as the United

Nations, the G20, the European Union and leading international companies, institutes and foundations use the term "circular economy" in all areas. The term "circular economy" was also used in the 1990s in the Chinese translation of the book *Cradle to Cradle* as part of the subtitle, so that, in China, Cradle to Cradle is often equated with the term circular economy.

Cradle to Cradle has already been featured in various museum exhibitions and internationally acclaimed documentaries. The support for Cradle to Cradle is growing: from the E.U.—e.g., the Belgian E.U. presidency—to China to the U.S.

Cradle to Cradle is generally regarded as the guiding path towards the global circular economy from the U.S. to the E.U. to China (see *The Green Industrial Revolution* by Woodrow W. Clark II & Grant Cooke, Butterworth-Heinemann, 2015, p. 368) as well as being the design philosophy at the heart of the circular economy (see *The Circular Economy – A Wealth of Flows* by Ken Webster, Ellen MacArthur

Foundation Publishing, 2017, p.16).

In the context of the groundbreaking *California Green Chemistry Initiative*, California Governor Arnold Schwarzenegger, in 2010, supported the launch of the C2C Products Innovation Institute (a U.S. non-profit organization managing the C2C certified Products program). One of the top recommendations of the California Environmental Protection Agency in 2008 was: "To Move Toward a Cradle-to-Cradle Economy." Today, California is the world's 5th-largest economy. Former U.S. President Bill Clinton wrote the foreword to Michael Braungart's and Bill McDonough's second book *The Upcycle.* The E.U. has funded several Cradle to Cradle projects like the international *Cradle to Cradle Network Project* (2010 - end of 2011), the international *Cradle to Cradle Islands Project* with partners from countries surrounding the North Sea (2009 - end of 2012) or, e.g., *BAMB* (Buildings as Material Banks, beginning 2015), a project that integrates C2C concepts in the building sector. China took inspiration from Cradle to Cradle for, e.g., its *Circular*

Economy Law in 2008. The World Economic Forum substantively embraced Cradle to Cradle methodologies in 2014 for its *Project Mainstream* to scale up the circular economy.

More and more governments and government agencies, as well Hollywood greats, musicians and fashion designers, entrepreneurs and cities like San Francisco or Venlo in the Netherlands are employing C2C principles. Venlo, for example, uses C2C techniques in its city hall to help to purify the air. A wide assortment of foundations, organizations, universities, and people around the world, support the groundbreaking Cradle to Cradle design concept. It allows people to be good and positive to themselves as well as to nature, to celebrate creativity, abundance and thus infinite possibilities along with diversity and beauty. In short, Cradle to Cradle enables people to be happy about their own existence!

"Nature operates according to a system of nutrients and metabolisms in which there is no such thing as waste."
Michael Braungart & William McDonough
(Cradle to Cradle, Vintage, 2009, p.92)

"I've watched as many of the concepts presented in *Cradle to Cradle* have taken root at the U.S. Postal Service and NASA (…) and in countries around the world. I've seen how these simple ideas, when put into practice, can improve productivity and make people happier and healthier."
U.S. President Bill Clinton
(Foreword to The Upcycle by William McDonough and Michael Braungart, 2013, p. xvii)

"If we are to succeed (…) it is very important to develop a circular economy based on cradle-to-cradle principles (…) what China's government wants to achieve."
Madame Deng Nan,
China's Party Secretary for Science and Technology
(as quoted in Sense & Sustainability by Ken Webster and Craig Johnson, 2008, p. 29)

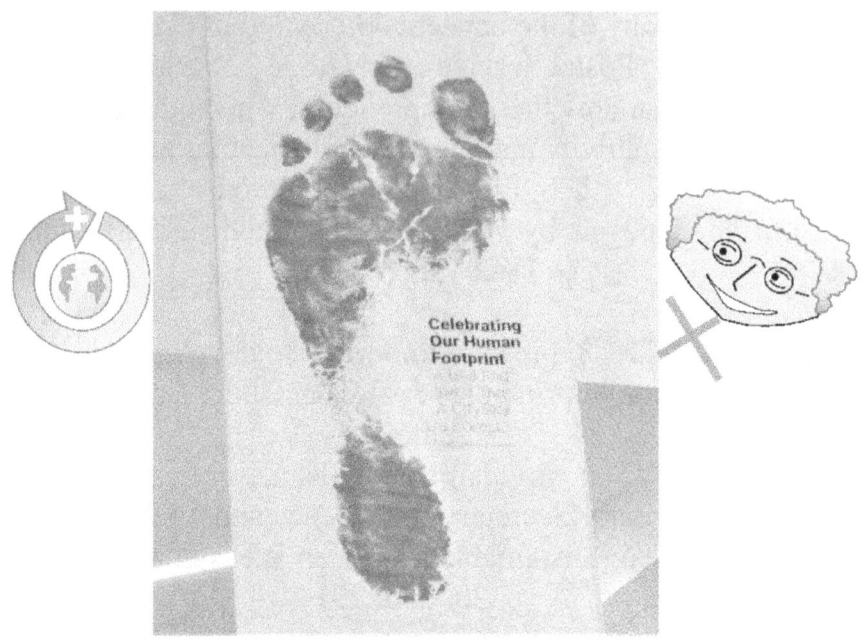

THE POSITIVE FOOTPRINT

**The huge poster of the C2C exhibition at the Biennale
Architettura 2016 in Venice,
presented in the lobby of the Libeskind-Building during the C2C Congress
2017.**

Celebrating
Our Human
Footprint

A Building
like a Tree
A City like
a Forest

Michael Braungart's Idea:

with the help of the C2C design concept based on the cyclic scheme of Nature, humanity can create a positive, growing ecological footprint, that everyone can be happy about.

Inspirations from Michael Braungart's life for the story
C2C GALAXY:

• For the Cradle to Cradle design concept, Michael Braungart was inspired by the example of nature as well as from various branches of science and the humanities and from different eras and cultural environments from all over the world. Various aspects of human existence, such as joy, fantasy, beauty or meaningfulness, also belong to Cradle to Cradle.

• Michael Braungart once fell in love with his chemistry teacher during his school years, and to woo her...

• ...he taught the whole class chemistry!

• His parents had a colorful, joyfully growing garden, for which they first had to pay a fine and then later got an award for it.

• Michael Braungart loves to use humor in his lectures.

• He loves using ants as an example for humankind because they're so intelligent and cooperate together so well and live constructively with nature.

• He thinks the cherry tree is a wonderful example from nature for positive abundance, from which the environment benefits.

• C2C is not about being "less bad to the environment and to oneself", but rather about designing and optimizing things to be positive for humans and the planet from the start, so that the human, ecological footprint can always keep growing for the benefit of people and the environment.

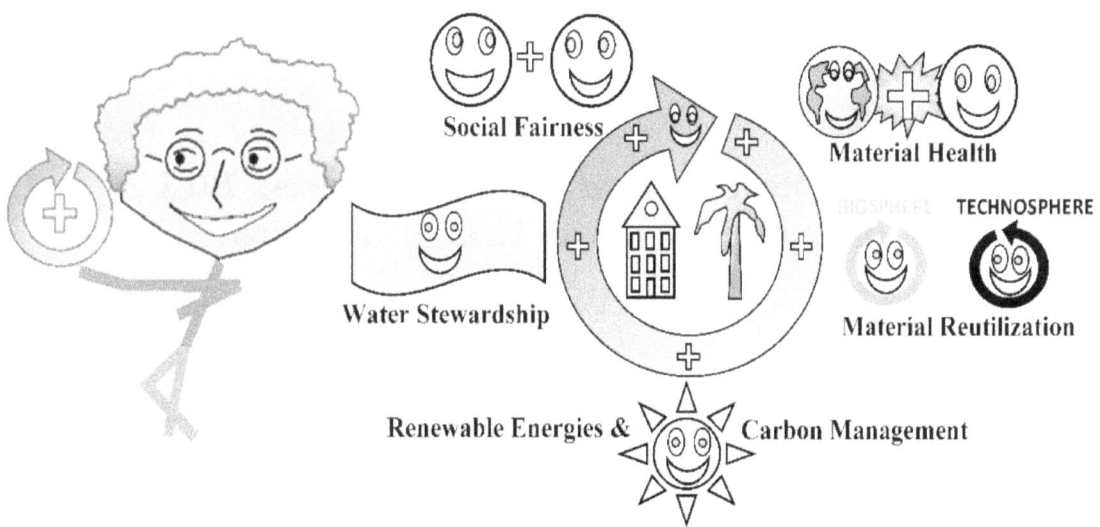

THE 5 C2C PRINCIPLES

"There is no zero waste. It's all nutrient."

**Michael Braungart at the C2C Congress 2017
(in an interview with George Hohbach)**

**"We can look to Nature (…) as our teacher. Nature gave us
the correct recipe."
Michael Braungart & William McDonough
(The Upcycle, North Point Press, 2013, p.221)**

CRADLE TO CRADLE: MISSION "POSITIVE, CIRCULAR UNITY OF NATURE"

From the scientific findings of Albert Einstein regarding the core role of **local symmetry** in Nature or epigenetics (molecular biology/cell biology) it follows that nature understands itself as a unity (everything is inextricably interwoven). Unity (holistic wholeness, quality) is POSITIVE (a plus), as a missing part would mean less unity, that is a (negative) minus. In addition, unity always means equality (balance, harmony, beauty, symmetry). This is the concept of the equation, which states that two aspects are identical (equal, symmetric). The result is the natural, positive-nourishing dynamic of the cycle that transforms the aspects of the equation: one aspect into the other—such as in the equation which forms the C2C basis:

Even on the smallest level—the level of quantum mechanics—**local symmetry** causes the interactions between fundamental particles (quanta) and, therefore, also cosmic evolution.

CRADLE TO CRADLE aims at translating and implementing Nature's core principle of **local symmetry** as a coherent, circular system for humankind.

LOCAL SYMMETRY RULES! and creates a global, symmetric (balanced, harmonious) UNITY-NETWORK throughout the entire cosmos and, therefore, here on planet Earth, too. LOCAL CYCLES form a global, balanced (symmetric) unity-network of circularity producing BIODIVERSITY (abundance) on planet Earth.

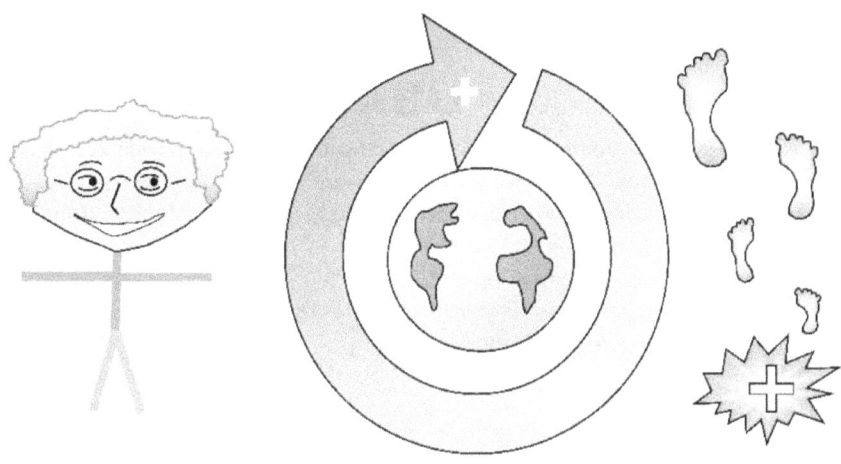

THY **C2C** CYCLES OF THE BIO- & TECHNOSPHERE

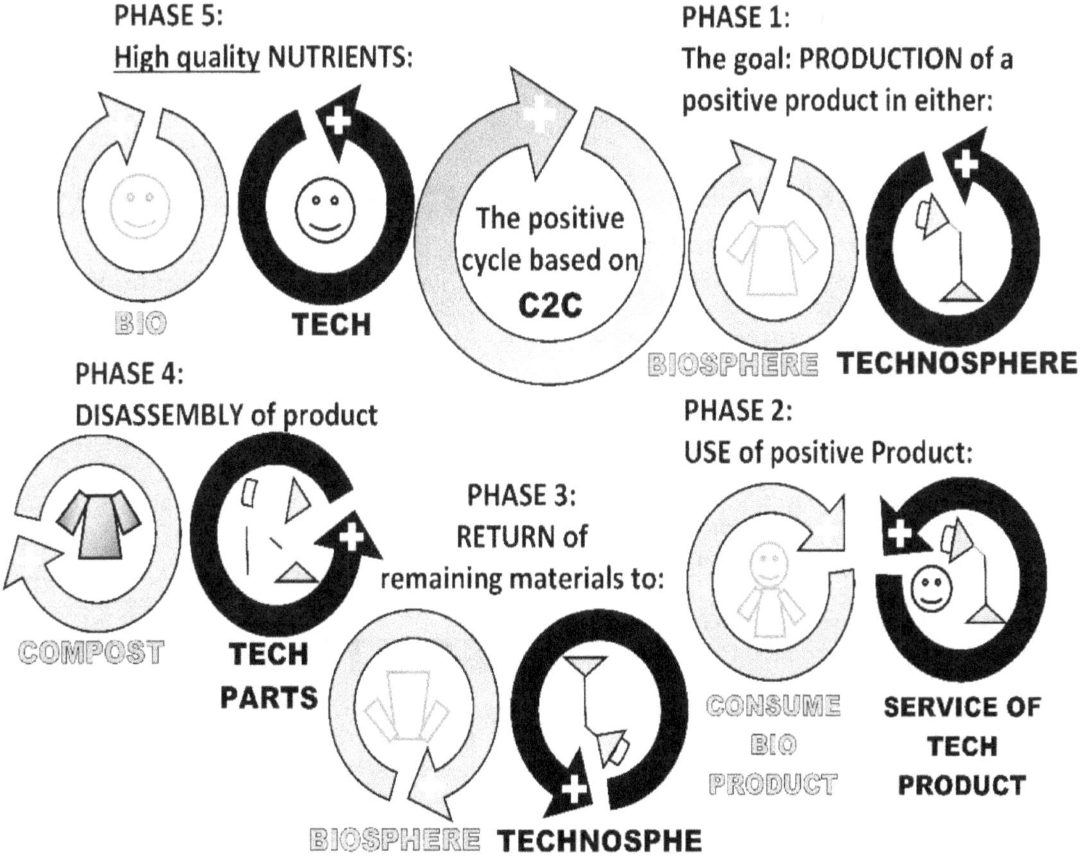

PHASE 5:
High quality NUTRIENTS:

BIO   **TECH**

The positive cycle based on **C2C**

PHASE 1:
The goal: PRODUCTION of a positive product in either:

BIOSPHERE   **TECHNOSPHERE**

PHASE 4:
DISASSEMBLY of product

COMPOST   **TECH PARTS**

PHASE 3:
RETURN of remaining materials to:

BIOSPHERE   **TECHNOSPHE**

PHASE 2:
USE of positive Product:

CONSUME BIO PRODUCT   **SERVICE OF TECH PRODUCT**

C2C: Eco-Intelligence Goes Global

USA:

- California's former Governor Arnold Schwarzenegger supports C2C.
- US President Bill Clinton writes the foreword for the book *The Upcycle*.
- EPA (US Environmental Protection Agency) recommends the C2C standard.
- San Francisco uses the C2C Standard.
- Many Hollywood greats support C2C.
- The C2C Products Innovation Institute helps to scale the C2C idea.
- Many US companies implement C2C.

  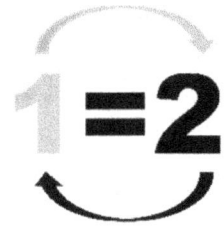

EU:

- EU-funded, international projects like:
  - The C2C Network Project
  - The C2C Islands Project
  - BAMB (Buildings as Material Banks)
- Many regional C2C projects
- Venlo, the C2C region
- The *Cradle to Cradle NGO* informs the public & organizes the annual, international *C2C Congress*.
- The Ellen MacArthur Foundation uses C2C principles to promote the Circular Economy worldwide.
- The World Economic Forum refers to C2C for its circular-economy project "Mainstream".
- Many exhibitions like the *Expo 2000* in Hannover or award-winning documentaries like *Waste=Food* present C2C.
- Many companies implement C2C.

CHINA & ASIA:

- The international bestseller *Cradle to Cradle* is also a huge success in China. The book was published by the Chinese government and universities. The subtitle of the Chinese version was "The Design of the Circular Economy".
- China borrows heavily from C2C for its Circular Economy Law in 2008.
- Several companies in Asia implement C2C.

CENTRAL & SOUTH AMERICA

- *The Hannover Principles* serve as the foundation for Cradle to Cradle and are presented to the 1992 Earth Summit's World Urban Forum in Rio de Janeiro, Brazil.
- Bionutrient recycling projects get implemented in Central and South America.
- Several companies implement C2C.

104

The source of inspiration for this novel

Michael Braungart

is the internationally renowned, award-winning co-founder of the groundbreaking Cradle to Cradle design concept. He is a chemistry professor, multiple bestselling author, sought-after speaker and the founder and CEO of EPEA (Environmental Protection Encouragement Agency), the international research and consulting institute for Cradle to Cradle solutions and their implementation. Throughout the world, companies in all fields, are—thanks to C2C—increasingly succeeding in designing and manufacturing products in an environmentally-intelligent way that benefits both humans and the environment. For many years now, C2C has received continuous support from numerous Hollywood greats and celebrities around the world. More and more governments, government agencies, regions, cities and organizations rely on C2C to achieve improvements for humans and planet. For this book and the story, Michael Braungart was the source of inspiration with his life, his thoughts and his work.

The authors

George Hohbach

studied law and has collaborated for many years with a talent and literary agency in Beverly Hills. His art—music, paintings, books, documentaries—is presented domestically and abroad in galleries, educational centers, companies and museums. On the systematic connection between Albert Einstein's revolutionary and groundbreaking, scientific discovery regarding the core role of simple, beautiful and local symmetry in Nature, i.e., in the cosmos, and the symmetric, nature-based Cradle to Cradle design principle he has written numerous system-theoretical analyses, a summary of which was published by a science publisher. He is the head writer of this novel, illustrated the 2nd part of the book and wrote both the music and lyrics for the novel's title song *C2C GALAXY* and the theme song *C2C Circular Economy*.

Ehrengard Hohbach

is a former physician with a specialty in holistic medicine. She gave numerous lectures, seminars and courses on that topic. Her expressionist, symbolic paintings— also inspired by C2C and Einstein's findings about symmetry—are exhibited in galleries, companies and museums domestically and abroad. Her artistic and literary work was covered several times on radio programs as well as in newspaper articles.

Scott Marcano

is the critically acclaimed and award-winning writer/director/producer and CEO of Diablo Productions. His film and television credits include movies for MGM and The Walt Disney Company, including the cult environmental comedy *Bio-Dome*. For this book, he was also the project manager.

The illustrator

Juan Romera

is a well-known illustrator from Argentina who is working with publishers around the world. He has also collaborated on several critically-acclaimed graphic novels with Diablo Comics.

The Co-Translator

Robin Palmer

is a veteran Hollywood agent, producer and television network executive who has worked in the business for over 30 years. Robin Palmer is also a produced screenwriter and has published numerous Young Adult novels with Penguin Random House and Simon & Schuster. She currently resides in Louisiana where she teaches in the film department of Tulane University.

The Musician

Alfred Huff

is a well-known German musician, film music composer and the CEO of Medienhaus Mainz. He worked on the final production of the sheet music of *C2C GALAXY* & *C2C Circular Economy* as well as on the arrangement of the novel's songs and their recording.

ACKNOWLEDGMENTS:

Such a book does not come into existence without the enthusiastic participation of many people. But we wish to single out a few here: First of all, many thanks to Prof. Braungart for allowing us to write the book based on his life and groundbreaking ideas. Many thanks to Gülcan Yurt, office manager at EPEA, for the always friendly and warm support, as well as to Patrick Meiß, personal advisor to Prof. Braungart. Many thanks also to both our inspiring project manager Scott Marcano, our imaginative illustrator Juan Romera and our most supportive musician Alfred Huff for their productive collaboration and to author Robin Palmer for her excellent help with the English translation. Finally, our thanks to our agent Lloyd Robinson for the comprehensive support of the project.

Appendix

Cradle to Cradle
& Albert Einstein's Findings About Symmetry

Cradle to Cradle (C2C):

The design concept by chemist Michael Braungart and architect William McDonough is based on the recognition that Nature understands itself as a unity. This unity or wholeness of Nature shows itself, e.g., in holistic unity-cycles, like Nature's diverse and countless nutrient cycles. C2C uses two different such unity-cycles, a nutrient cycle for the biosphere of nature and one for the technosphere, the realm of man-made technology. Since both seemingly different C2C cycles are structured the same way and have the same goal—namely, to design and produce things in an environmentally intelligent way so that they are positive for humans and the planet right from the start—the C2C holistic unity-cycles, and thus also the products, form a scientifically based, simple, harmonic and, therefore, symmetrical whole. Since chemistry plays a connective role between physics, biology and other fields of science, it has the potential—as in C2C—to translate basic natural laws into positive-holistic concepts for humankind.

Albert Einstein:

The physicist Albert Einstein was born in Ulm (Germany) in 1879 and died in 1955 in Princeton, USA. From a very early age he was interested in mathematics and spent long hours studying the field with a family friend. At age 12, he became convinced that Nature (the cosmos) could be understood as a simple mathematical structure. With the help of **local symmetry** (sameness, equality, equivalence, unity, balance, invariance, i.e., remaining unchanged, harmony) as a simple, beautiful, mathematical idea—scientifically discovered in Nature—Einstein later achieved his groundbreaking successes of the theories of relativity. These theories, based on local symmetry as the core principle of Nature (the cosmos), created a unified, harmonious understanding of the entire universe in which the local laws of Nature are the same for all observers. One of Einstein's great achievements was that he took simplicity seriously and revealed this elegance, i.e., beauty in Nature. At first, Einstein wanted to give his theory of relativity the title *Invariance Theory* because *invariance* represents "remaining unchanged", i.e., "staying the same" and thus stands for symmetry.

The well-known mathematician **Emmy Noether** (1882-1952) underpinned the fact that the local laws of Nature are always invariant (symmetric, the same) and thus also confirmed Einstein's findings and the significance of local symmetry in Nature. Einstein called Emmy Noether the most important woman in the history of mathematics.

The discoveries of Einstein, which provide the foundation for a scientifically-based, modern holistic view of Nature (the cosmos and our home planet Earth), are built on the findings of **Galileo Galilei** (1564-1642)—who also began to scientifically reveal the importance of sameness or symmetry in Nature—and **Isaac Newton** (1643-1727).

For Einstein, fantasy and imagination were even more important than knowledge, and he described the mysterious in Nature as the most beautiful experience and as both a fundamental feeling and as the source of science and art alike. The various disciplines which—according to Einstein—should enrich the life of every human individual, he saw as the branches of a single tree.

In addition, symmetry considerations also point to the oneness of Nature (the cosmos) on the level of quantum mechanics.

"Based on our experiences so far, we have reason to be confident that nature is the realization of the simplest conceivable mathematical concept."
Albert Einstein
(On the Method of Theoretical Physics, 10 June 1933, Author translation)

"... Albert Einstein (...) brought a new style into thinking about Nature's fundamental principles. For Einstein beauty, in the specific form of symmetry, takes on a life of its own. Beauty becomes a creative principle."
Frank Wilczek
(A Beautiful Question, 2015, p.199)

"... symmetry is the underlying and most important theme of nature."
Leon M. Lederman & Christopher T. Hill
(Symmetry and the Beautiful Universe, 2004, p.73)

Further Reading

C2C:

- *Cradle to Cradle* by Michael Braungart & William McDonough, Vintage, 2009
- *The Upcycle* by Michael Braungart & William McDonough, North Point Press, 2013
- *Creating Buildings with Positive Impact* by Douglas Mulhall, Michael Braungart & Katja Hansen, Technical University of Munich, 2013

C2C inspired Circular Economy, Environment, Climate:

- *Completing the Picture – How The Circular Economy Tackles Climate Change*, a report by the Ellen MacArthur Foundation, 2019
- *The Green Industrial Revolution* by Woodrow W. Clark II & Grant Cooke, Butterworth-Heinemann, 2015

Circular Economy & the UN's 17 Sustainable Development Goals:

- *Why Symmetry Runs the Positive Circular Economy* by George Hohbach, BoD, 2021
- *The Circular Economy – A User's Guide* by Walter Stahel, Routledge, 2019
- *The Circular Economy – A Powerful Force for Climate Mitigation*, a report by Material Economics and its partners
- *Closing the Loop – The benefits of the circular economy for developing countries and emerging economies* by Alexandre Gobbo Fernandes, a project by EPEA Brasil, Tearfund, NuRes, Tearfund, 2016
- *The Trillion Dollar Shift – Achieving the Sustainability Goals* by Marga Hoek, Routledge, 2018

Albert Einstein:

- *Ideas and Opinions* by Albert Einstein, Three Rivers Press
- *Einstein – His Life and Universe* by Walter Isaacson, Simon & Schuster, 2008

Galileo, Newton and other great Scientists:
- *From Galileo to Gell-Mann* by Marco Bersanelli & Mario Gargantini, Templeton Press, 2009
- *Newton's Gift* by David Berlinski, Touchstone, 2000
- *Physics & Philosophy* by Werner Heisenberg, Harper Perennial, 2007

Symmetry (advanced level):
Note: physicists often refer to symmetry (equivalence, sameness, balance, harmony) as invariance
- *Relativity – The Special & The General Theory* by Albert Einstein, Martino Publishing, 2010
- *Symmetry and the Beautiful Universe by* Leon Lederman and Christopher Hill, Prometheus Books, 2004
- *A Beautiful Question* by Frank Wilczek, Allen Lane, 2015
- *Symmetry – A Journey into the Patterns of Nature* by Marcus du Sauttoy, Harper Perennial, 2009
- *Love & Math* by Edward Frenkel, Basic Books, 2013

Holism & Harmony/Balance with Nature:
- *A System Change Compass*, co-authored by The Club of Rome and SYSTEMIQ, 2020
- *Harmony – A New Way of Looking at Our World* by HRH The Prince of Wales, HarperCollins*Publishers*, 2010
- *Drawdown – The Most Comprehensive Plan Ever Proposed To Reverse Global Warming* edited by Paul Hawken, Penguin Books, 2017
- *Leonardo da Vinci* by Walter Isaacson, Simon & Schuster, 2017
- *Rethinking Humanity* by James Arbib & Tony Seba, RethinkX, 2020
- *The Invention of Nature* by Andrea Wulf, John Murray, 2015

Epigenetics:
- *The Biology of Belief* by Bruce Lipton, Hay House, 2015
- *Molecules of Emotion* by Candace Pert, Simon & Schuster, 1997

Also by George Hohbach & Ehrengard Hohbach with Scot Marcano; illustrations by Juan Romera:

C2C NOVEL
MICHAEL & MIA
An Adventure in the Positive Cycle of Nature
illustrated Middle Grade Novel

Two young chemistry fans, haunted by a polluting, mad robot, discover a stunning, circular solution in Nature at the last minute that can save their home planet.

A humorous adventure based on the life of C2C co-founder Michael Braungart with background information on the school of thought of C2C.
Plus: the theme song *NATURE LIVES* as sheet music.

C2C NOVEL
AGENT C2C
Positive for People and Planet
illustrated Young Adult Action-Comedy Novel

Agent C2C and his two American cohorts have to find solutions to two dangerous international crises and the growing environmental challenges – fast!

A humorous action adventure based on the life of C2C co-founder Michael Braungart with background information on the school of thought of C2C. Plus: the title song *AGENT C2C* as sheet music.

C2C

POP SONGS

& YouTube Videos
Music & lyrics by George Hohbach

♪

C2C GALAXY
AGENT C2C
NATURE LIVES
C2C CIRCULAR ECONOMY

Follow George Hohbach also on
Instagram: @georgehohbach
Twitter: @GHohbach
Spotify, Amazon Music, Apple Music, Deezer, Napster

LET'S GO FULL CYCLES!